Path from

Poverty to a

Business Owner

Walkthrough

Introduction

Life as we know has two paths. You can either go up or you can keep going up. Nobody wants to go down. Let's face it, it's one of the dreadest failures any human faces in the economic world that we live in. And what I mean by economic world, is that no matter what the cost we cannot simply avoid settling for the same modern way of life. Which is one of the biggest obstacles for retirement. Many of us want to settle. Yet, there's simply no way of knowing what the outcome will be. So, I discovered a solution to this enormous dread of continuous economic prosperity, which is starting a business with little costs.

Starting a business on the side is ultimately in the long run a life-saving retirement plan. Although you may feel that owning a business is intimidating. What I have entailed is that once you get started the feeling of failure is no longer a concern it becomes a destiny. A destiny set foot to provide a survival blanket for you or what matters to you the most. Keep in mind that all businesses suffer a loss or a gain, shareholders, business partners and even investors. More importantly than all of these assets, is a customer. A customer is what each business needs in order to facilitate a successful business operation.

Success of your business is not based on money as the primary factor but as the lifespan of the business. Meaning, a business is only profitable by the amount of years it can remain stable. As long as you understand what is keeping the economy constantly growing. Comprehending this method to withstand a successful business is the blue print to your business plan.

Getting Started

Starting a business is essentially an easy enrollment to start the process of eliminating stacks of poverty. So, let's begin, with the business name. Decide on a name that you feel strongly confident about. You can change the font and make it look cool in Word for free. Even if you choose a name that someone already has, because at this point it's hardly accomplishable to avoid. You can still add or edit the name so as long as it does not run into trademark issues in that specific category. What does this mean? If another business has the name Integrity and you select a name Integrity Commercial Cleaning then as long as it's in two different categories, they're should be no complications. However, when discussing trademark issues, you should consult a business lawyer. Most of the time, lawyers provide a free consultation, before suggesting working with you. Which is very beneficial because lawyers can prepare you on what obstacles you may come across in business. Because anything initially that you create can be licensed and sold to another entity for profit. Such as creating an instrumental beat and selling it for background music. In today's algorithm (a path that leads to a popular content or a specific task), there are many platforms that will distribute this request to reach a certain customer or market. If you can remember a dance that was created, this would be an example of a creation that you can trademark or get paid for creating because you are the one who created the content that people are utilizing.

Trademark

Let's face it, we all want to protect our invention of some sort. Although once you create or invent something, it is suggested that it is yours. Even though getting a trademark is so that you can protect overtime anyone deciding to take the name of your brand, you still have time to pay for it. Initially, your brand overtime is what increases your sales tremendously because of how many people see the name. I am sure you can think of a soda company that has a brand name on almost all of their products they sell. Not to mention the first product had to make a statement. From my considerable understanding of a trademark, is that if you plan to create a product that you want to stand for a purpose, a trademark protects someone from taking the name and what it represents for you or your business.

A trademark is not something to necessarily focus too much on unless you have an idea or invention you want to protect expeditiously. Ensuring a provisional patent will protect your idea. Which is under a $100 dollars last time I checked. Although anyone can still steal your idea by way of just modification, don't let it stop you. Because once you actually apply for a provisional patent, you are securing your rights to sell your idea to a company, contrary to selling a new invented service or product. Just in case a company does steal your invention, you can later higher an attorney to seek your rights to claiming property of the invention. A trademark would generally benefit someone who is seeking to protect the name of something new that is unheard of.

Provisional Patent

A provisional patent protects your idea for a short period (12 months) of time until you have all the prototypes, funding or securing the manufacturing of what you intend to use a provisional patent. That's when it gets expensive. Which is why inventors work so hard to get the word out to investors. An example of getting a provisional patent would be, if you wanted to patent a name for the use of branding for the leveraging of marketing the description of an invention per say. For instance, say you like a particular brand or application. If you have an idea of how this invention will benefit another company, you can sell your invention. For allot of money depending on the return on investment it could bring the company and you. You can do this by getting the provisional patent so you can protect your description of how this invention will operate. Create a marketing package fit to that specific company. Arrange a meeting with the manager or the person that makes decisions about the companies spending budget. Discuss in the meeting with a packet introducing your project and prototype. From there I would say you may need a business lawyer to negotiate the contract or to even make sure your contacting this company strategically. Or someone experienced in sales. So, if you are in the market of selling your idea to another business in order to provide that business with a profitable idea, getting a provisional patent is a great idea to bargain your invention so you can protect your asset.

Copyright

Along with getting a provisional patent in which leads to an actual patent is getting a copyright. Copyright generally protects the authentication of authorship of one's work, literary, musical or computer software. Also known as Intellectual Property, defined as something created in the mind: Divided into two categories. Industrial property and geographical indications. It's safe to safe if you wanted to develop a computer software you would have to file for a copyright which can be done online. Basically, the moment you make something and establish yourself as the owner to that publication (poetry, book, article, movie, musical, songs, computer software, and architecture) the only way to sue is if the work is filed and copyrighted. Even after your publication has been copyrighted, let's say someone copies your song or uses your words as their invention. Filing an application for copyright protects your words, even after it has been infringed upon. It's recommended to ask a legal qualified representative to state whether your invention would need to be copyrighted. Yet and still, this is directed for the works of publication of ones' intellectual property. For instance, if you were to create a specific dance and it goes viral, it would be best to know how to protect what you created. Furthering that gift of luck, have a way for any media to contact you from where it was posted of course. Just keep in mind if that happens ensure you are noted as the creator of the viral content.

Online and offline strategy

What many of us are doing now with the popularity of social media is practicing are business skills of customer engagement. Unfortunately, if you think about it, social media is a way to connect with millions of people to get approval about a particular idea or expression. Everyone is constantly posting, engaging and commenting on something that affects their personal feelings. The channels to pay for advertising your product or services depend on a which social media platform works best in targeting to the right customers of course. Which has worked for many online business owners. Even if it was podcast, essentially, targets to a specific demographic (age, gender, likes, etc.) on the social media. Which is a great marketing approach for selling an independent service business online. Independent online businesses that our trending such as a podcast, YouTube channel, blogging, drop shipping, and reselling benefit from targeted ads on social media. However, it would depend on if you can spend 5 dollars for 3 to 5 days to reach a target-customers to lead them to what your offering with just a click of a link. Essentially, turning them into customers. There are even video templates to assist you in creating your video ad if you already have video footage. Or pay a freelancer to gather video ad clips to import a small video ad for customers to engage in at best. You want customers to like, trust and engage in your video ad and click to check out the exciting offer. Remembering as a business offering deals to customers is a very effective ad and not to mention exciting to receive anything less than what we normally have to pay. Which is the actual retail price, lol.

The hard part executing an effective video ad is the feedback. Getting good reviews and creating a band wagon of great testimonials, from real accounts is challenging. Let's face it people tend to buy what everyone is ok with buying but also make false claims. Not to mention comments and likes. The other side of the band wagon is people thriving for good educational life-saving content. Providing, it helps people solve a problem is an effective way to build trust. I wouldn't suggest thinking overboard but more of keeping a steady acknowledgement of what customer satisfaction means to others. The best way to find an idea of that is simply asking yourself what things you would like to improve or what people have of interest of knowing. You'll have to create influencing in as many smart ways as possible of course. Meaning, you don't want to over-do-it, fake-it too much or rush anything you put out. Just make an announcement about what you are launching on a platform in a video format or clever short second watch if you're the person offering the service personally. If not disregard this last statement. Reason I say this is because customers rarely care who own the website. In fact, it's harder to get customers to buy from an owner based off that person's culture without being biased. That's the band wagon for you. It's better to keep it professionally focused on the business name and brand (which is what it stands for). This way you can drive traffic to a click link. A link that sends customers to which is considered a landing page or whatever you want people to discover what your providing a business to do. The best way to continue reaching these leads turns into a sales channel. By creating a way for visitors to leave their email address for a discount in a popup form maturely works. So that you can send updates on upcoming deals and sales by email. There are also email format you can use to apply a mass email to send to customers. This is called email marketing. Mostly this is effective when someone actually buys from you to get them to come back again. A little creativeness in the way you offer a discount can assist in customer engagement. However, this only applies for making an online business. If you try to do the most it could potentially decay the reputation of the business and your brand.

Although, this may sound like some overwhelming step process or as if you're a puppet because you have to work around the heavy stereotypes and competition on social media just to make a impact it is the same as offline. Single handedly, all businesses face these same occurrences. What works the best is observing what other businesses are doing. For instance, you want to sell a product and you want a lot of people to become aware about it because they need it, you don't want to create the same urgency as your competitor. Yours' has to be uniquely different. Think of it like you are in the bread aisle, all bread is identical but, it's packaged and branded differently.

Brand Model

The most popular forms of spreading awareness in my eyes of your product is the brand marketing method. Depending on what your business is offering, is what determines your avenue of brand marketing. Ultimately encouraging your customers to shop with you is the format of executing their trust and consistency. Attending business expos, games or events can also help exposure as a side note. Generally, depending on what you are trying to sell. It gives you an open mind of what to expect. If you were anticipating a new product you developed or have a prototype for, this would be a way to get your foot in the door and see what your competition is. Expos are found in the events section in the local chapter, event space or Eventbrite that provides seekers a way to meetup within close proximity in every city. Checking around your Chamber of Commerce offices will lead you to the contacts that initiate expos. Simply so you can ask questions of where they would be held. You never know, you may want to hold your own business expo and get other business minded individuals to come together. Of course, having an idea of what goes on during a event that you are seeking to have is best so you can know if that would be a good fit for you.

Advertise Model

Is it simple to just pay for promotion of what your selling? Quite frankly, Yes! Just think about it when you listen to the radio, how many commercials you hear? How many times it plays for you to remember the name and what they're selling? Well, newspapers, podcast, Facebook, social media advertising and simple indirect and direct mail is of the many way to pay for promotion. Email marketing are very clever engagements that send notifications to subscribers' phones. It let's them know instantly what they need to know instantly. Just like if you wanted to know if your favorite shoes were dropping soon, you want to get ready to make that purchase. Typically, the most popular spending times surround the bi-weekly, payroll structure. You have the ability to add links and place copy ads (a picture promoting a product or service) in the email to create clicks as well. Which simply sends that person to what your selling. Unless you want to pay for google ad which can be costly if you don't know what you are doing. Meaning it's easy to spend way too much money advertising with no return on investment. Advertising is paid for when someone clicks on the link. The objective is to get the customer driven enough to buy what they have interest in. Although it's worth it to pay for ads, you have to target to the right customers and watch the ad campaign of how many customers are actually turning into sales.

To start off I would promote in the area that your wanting to find customers. For instance, if your selling T-shirts, you would simply create ads to sell T-shirts in your city, community, school, area etc. Maybe one or 3 cool shirts if you will and put a sale on it, creates click potential. Work on searchable key words that pertain to the product your selling or service keywords when your putting in the description of the item. Keep it structured the way a person goes about searching for that item. Checking into local newspapers is a low budget very effective promotional campaign as well to find customers. You are simply putting the word out there for whatever your selling in front of all newspaper readers. They should typically run the ad for 30 days or less. If you are wanting to establish an entertainment career this will also get the word out as well. Popular podcasts even have accessible ways of promoting your business with the revenue of getting commercials placed on the show. Most of them will create the ad for you or you can get a freelancer to get a script together depending how many words you get, which is sought with the actual podcast or radio host show fee. Facebook ads can be set by the age, area demographic etc. Same thing for YouTube with just 10 or 5 dollars a day, weekend, or it can be spread out evenly over the month. If you are unsure of what you want your ad to look like, just look at the competitive market you are in. To get an idea on how you may want your advertising to look like. For instance, the color size, or if you want it to be funny. Think about what you may have saw that made you want to buy the things you want is the secret to getting customers. Again, a freelancer can simplify this for a small budget fee, so you can spread your ad across whatever ad campaign and wait for the results.

Also expand your distribution ideas to just about everywhere you can think of that has advertising placement available for your specific customer. Even at bus stations or bulletin boards you can post flyers or coupons. In so many ways, depending on the specific business determines the best course of wording your advertising. In my opinion, I would keep a advertising budget at hand to keep money in reserve to ensure you can buy certain items or equipment to get things started. As you make a profit is when you will see the opportunity to take your profits to pay for more advertisement to customers. So, you can worry less about rushing to buy equipment in the beginning, until you actually get a service agreement with the customer. You can also decide on what to buy affordably from how much you will get paid. So, in case you need to get inventory that you need to acquire for the job require a small deposit or upfront fee. Find out the advertising costs and the duration of advertising as you rule out the least expensive to most. Watching a YouTube video is a simpler route to take if you still need to visualize the aspects of what these marketing channels do for customers. Sometimes it helps to see someone else execute a process that you never seen, before taking a leap of confidence in paying for results.

Many go all out there way to pay for promotion and receive little return on investment. Although it's stated scared money doesn't make money, neither does a bad investment. Setting wise restrictions on your money is the best way to ensure a safety blanket for testing out your marketing.

During downtimes, using phonebooks, past business cards, old emails to give you leads to finding more customers. You may even find customers on the bulletin board as your looking to advertise. Again, it's just based off of what you have a passion for.

(One day, I met this 10 Grade female in the library at a school I was visiting. And she showed me drawings that she wanted my advice on how much she could make from selling it. My response was you can set your own price, just make sure you are not too competitive.)

Prices too high can make the business lose profit. As I mentioned in the beginning, there's a profit and gain in all business. If you can think of a famous fast food restaurant that is not open on Sunday's, then you can see the way a loss and gain can play into your profit but yet as long as customers appreciate the value of business it's not a loss. In this case, the 10th grader would have to find places to sell her pictures at other stores that do consignments. And thus, split the profit from the selling of her painting.

Forming the Business

Now that you have an understanding of how to get customers through advertising, let's take a look at what you need to do to form your business. After you decided on the name you want your business name to be. Check your google search to see the competition of your name. You want to make sure you can secure a domain name as well before or immediately after you ensure the name you want to go with can be registered. You don't want a name that is commonly being used. Keep in mind you want the business name to be marketable. Searching the state website that you are opening a business in to see if that name is being used by someone else is a solid way to research your options as well. Always make sure that you are not jeopardizing your company or your name by sounding the same as another business in the same industry. As a friendly note, you can always change the name of your business even after you came up with a name. You'll just have to change all the paperwork and branding. The hospital I gave birth to my son at changed their name due to a bad reputation of malpractice complaints from unexplained deaths. This only changed the perception of new patients, however not my memory of their reputation.

Depending on which city, state, county you live in may differentiates the process of getting registered but it's mostly pretty standard. You can register as a sole proprietor or LLC. Now of course there are other business entities, these are the two I say are the simplest. A sole proprietor is just what it says, you are the only owner. However, you can assign a manager, or hire an employee still under this category. They just have to get either a 1099 or later a W-2 which is established through payroll.

Simple Entity

The difference between an LLC and a sole proprietor is revealing the assets of the owner or owners, essentially protecting you from your business. The cost to register the business as a sole proprietor is usually half the cost of getting an LLC. An estimated cost of an LLC is about $125.00. Both can be registered on your states home. An LLC also requires articles of your business which is in description to registering the LLC. Definitely not difficult to accomplish since it's your business, an example of what it may need to look like will help smooth the process. Which you can search for an example online. As a sole proprietor you can create a DBA, depending on the state it can be $10-$50 dollars. Which means doing business as instead of your first and last name. Keep in mind it's public record once you register your business so, you want to know what address and phone number to list for your business. When registering your domain name for your business website, it will also show the person who registered the domain name, as a friendly reminder. However, you can pay to have it be listed private or it can be a virtual address I believe, just simply put the business address down you want to use and business name. You can use also use a Facebook like page as a free website or I prefer a google business profile website to start off free of charge. The google business profile allows customers to see your business is verified. You can use your own, royalty free photos or pay for photos to create a portfolio of services. As an idea, if you are having a hard time setting up your images on a website or business profile, you can have an image edited for a small fee depending on the freelance site you choose. What I mean by this, is say you have an ideal image or logo you want displayed to represent what your selling or providing a service for, you may need the photo edited or something created so that the picture makes sense to the business. I myself have kept under a budget, utilizing freelancers to work with me for little needs such as a logo. Of course, it wasn't until later, did I want a professional logo, simply because I used a clip art image from Word and made it into a small figure to add to shorten the business name, initially. Finding simple photos was not hard, I just simply searched the internet for royalty free photos. Businesses like a commercial cleaner, pictures of the previous services are questionable anyway, so cleaners have to stand by the word to prove their work is consistent. Some people pay thousands for a website for their business. When others create a website using the simplest photos to match the product or service with just a simple description to match the customers' needs. When you put it in reality, there are certain services you do not care how special their website is, such as a landscaping business, you just need someone to come right away.

A freelance product editor could work the images up to make it look more hi-def depending on what your selling or providing a service for. For example, a barber would need nice photos unless there are images of haircuts displayed so customers can decide what cut to choose from. Some businesses pay people to take pictures for their business to promote as well. Making their website stand out from its' competitors. I would take the easiest route in collecting royalty free or personal photos before getting started just to keep things all under budget. Ensure you create blogs of any news about your business for when customers are searching for those specific services. Reason I mention this is because, you could possibly stumble across an article related to a search about a particular area that describes the services you offer to help solve that problem. Testimonials are also a plus to add to your website. Why? Because it creates a trust for customers that other customers are satisfied with doing business with you. You could ask people you know to rate your business and leave a review just to play it safe. That way you feel more confident receiving tips from people you know. Giving customers referral bonuses or gift certificates is a good way to maintain customer loyalty. You would just simply print some discounts that you can either create or copy an image idea and change it to your business. Again, I can't stress this enough, you want to establish trust and consistency for customers if you plan to have a good name for your business, offering discounts and gift certificates is a good way to make customer's feel confident in your service. Always remain professional online and offline if you are working your business using your own name. For instance, if you wanting to offer personal care services, you would want to maintain a image customers would want to trust you with their love ones. Also, this is another great idea to get a business started to offer personal care services and hiring a can to care for the residents that contact your business for services.

Business Vision

When you register your business name, DBA (doing business as), or LLC (limited liability corporation), its' time to ensure you have a business number and 800 number. Setup a free google email account for your business. Inside your settings, ensure that you add your business name and logo to your email signature in your email settings. That way it shows on all emails that you send and respond to, if you haven't seen this already. You can learn to send out auto responders and eventually handle your own email marketing when sending to more than one person at a time. This task is easy when your offering a deal, new item or service once customers start contacting you or you make contact with a potential customer. Order business cards and keep it simple in starting out phase by using a standard business card template. The purpose of the card is simply to give to a potential customer or after the service is granted so the customer can keep. This can cost around $10 to $20 dollars depending on the quantity. I started off with about 20 cards because I wasn't sure how many people I would run into personally. This can be printed at home if you have a hi-def printer or at a printing store which will cost of course 10 to 20 dollars. Otherwise, if you had your own personal printer, you would pay for the paper to actual print your business cards on. Order your name badge for meeting customers in person and again do not put owner or CEO on badge. You do not want to become a target. Just keep it simple to the position that you are acting in.

Business credit

You will need an EIN number that can be given to you free from the IRS website. The reason for an EIN number is so that you can separate your business credit and income from your own. Although personal credit plays an important role in obtaining business credit the EIN separates business credit from personal credit. Which is important when getting financed for business credit to expand. Obtaining an EIN establishes a business credit report with any loans. Note: you will need an EIN to open a business account. Say for instance someone writes you a check in your business name, a business bank account will allow you to cash and deposit the check or any other payment to the business. Depending on your credit when opening your business checking account, if your credit is fair applying for a business secured credit card would be my next step. When asked how much the business accumulates annually, provide with integrity that the business is essentially beginning with a few established service agreements or sales and that you basically intend to make a certain amount quarterly. Usually, gets the ball rolling. Like any credit, use with caution because, essentially you have to pay back that amount in order to expand operation if you haven't acquired the profit from your current business establishment. After 6 to 12 months business credit will have begun to show worthiness and that's when expansion comes in. You will be able to apply for a loan to expand your business. This could even mean opening up another store or such. However, you must know how to keep the business afloat or you could face severe backfire in obtaining credit. Just like personal credit when business credit reports a negative inquiry, it could affect the business financial reputation when it comes to investors and banks who want to see how well the business is doing. In case the business needs a loan for any reason, the business credit has established good history. My advice would be to keep as much money in reserve to raise your own bar.

Although, it's easier to just get money from the bank to start your business, growing the business with your own money and ambition insures customers that you care about your brand and they should too. One of the reasons is so that customers are safe and covered from liabilities if anything was to happen when your providing a service. This too runs a small monthly fee for when providing handyman services, if you are wanting to start a business as a trade. Now if you wanted to say start a business name to hire people to go out, let's say fix air conditioners. The term for this business is called a HVAC business, because a HVAC license is required by the technician, but not the owner. The owner again is simply the person who the business name is under. The services and jobs performed can be held by another title or profession. In this case, a person who holds a license to conduct the specific job.

Customers tend to feel comfortable with an insured business, because having bonded insurance, means this person has learned this trade. Being bonded secures the administration of doing business in schools, county libraries, and government entities. Even as an accountant, engineer etc., you are required to carry an E&O policy. Just in case the business is a professional establishment such as an accountant, error emission and omission covers' that profession. General business liability is the most common insurance that covers the general losses that may interrupt business such as a trip and fall, theft or fire customers intuition that this a good business to trust. If you were a cleaning company hired to clean at night, insurance on the business is why clients are going to trust you with their business at night. You must protect your business or the consequences of someone getting hurt on the job, especially other than you. Not being covered can cause serious damage to the company's lifespan. When you want to hire employees other than yourself, workers compensation is what you will need to carry in case one of your employees gets hurt on the job which is such a scary thing. Workers compensation is calculated by annual payroll so, there are low cost pay as you go packages available. Think of it as if you are paying a monthly subscription to your favorite podcaster. When starting a business, be mindful of the injuries that can occur so you can make the best decision on choosing the right insurance carrier to go through. As well as the employee, meaning ask questions about their health or if there's any medical problems that can cause injury. This is so you are not negligent of anything that can go wrong. A waiver form pre-printed can also be given to that employee. Also, knowing when you will be ready to hire employees and pay them will extend your coverage for worker's compensation insurance.

The Hustle

The hustle is when you are tied into a consistent project to carry out a specific task. When you wake up in the morning, whether it's to get the kids on the bus, ride share, delivery, or just anything that requires you to get up and carry out that task is a hustle. But in this case, you would just get up start early in the morning with emails. Sometimes opportunities and ideas can unexpectedly notify you with leads. For instance, you could possibly receive a email giving you a discount on equipment or an upcoming community. This is what you would call a lead because now you can target that area for business. Targeting an area is simply finding the customers that you are seeking to service or provide a product to sell to. Even if you are seeking to sell online, you can create SEO keywords specifically in that area for customers to find the best deals. And simply sell to that area online. If you perhaps wanted to provide a service for that area, it is also very effortless. So, as I mentioned previously about getting a google business page, you can change the location. Another way can be to simply say your simply servicing this area. You can also use that same approach on the phone when speaking with customers, that you are new to the area seeking to provide a service to their community. Simple as that. The conversation from that should go into further getting the details of the needs of the customers. With the help of technology, now a customer can send pictures of a site or need for what the service is for in case you have no way of arriving in-person to do an estimate. Depending on what the video or picture entails, a payment can be setup before or upon arrival to compensate your expenses of getting the job done.

If you would like, you can create your own invoice template on word and print it on carbon copy paper. Carbon copy paper is so that you can give the customer a copy initially. Carbon copy paper can initially be bought anywhere you would buy printing paper supply. If not, then customers can be sent an email that details a payment for them to use their credit card. In return, your account routing and bank number would be setup to receive payments from customers. Pay pal is what I started off with, which allowed me to setup my own personal account, so I could transfer money into an actually bank account. The importance of having some sort of bank account for your business is in case you need to provide business income for loans, taxes and developing partnerships. Lets' face it if you need someone to give you more money to expand the business, they would like to know how much money they would make from investing. Which essentially, is how investors starting at 500 to 50,000 would like to expand their money. This is what you would call passive income. Passive income is now something that you make back monthly, quarterly, or annually. Not only that you can reinvest money into another business and continue making the same thing. The disadvantage of this, is that it's a business. We all know that even the most popular businesses can go out of business. Just think of a car dealership that nobody does business with. Eventually, that car dealership will start either going out of business or offering all kinds of deals and expansion protection. Again, this is the hustle, the grind in having a business. Even a barber has to be contentious in keeping and finding clients.

If you wonder well, should I hire someone else to do this for me or help? How can I ensure the employee gets paid? Well surely, they will get paid on time through direct deposit from a pay roll service you set up with your bank or with a service (another business doing the same hustle as you) to pay the employee from the account that you get business income from. Which can be from a previous service you did on your own or reserve money. Depending on the service you provide the employee can be paid every week or commission. It sucks but we all have to go out to do a job first and unfortunately wait to get paid. So, just keep that in mind when discussing pay. Employee forms can be found easily on the internet, downloaded, printed signed and made copies of. Email can also be a source to send copies of electronic signature to. There are I believe software's' that allow electronic signature with the forms that you provide. It's just simply finding the right one you want to use after doing your research for that specific search result. So, let me put it into perspective, if you need to hire someone to setup a meeting, discuss the services for the business and that customer agrees to pay. Then that money would be the commission the employee would get. Either at the end of the week or bi-weekly. Your job would be to keep finding leads to ensure the calls are being made to these customers to get business. This is also extremely helpful when meetings can be overwhelming for owners who need a more energetic representative to meet with customers or clients.

The best way to do that is creating ads, flyers, regular mail or email to these businesses. The way to find them is by going to the state website where every business has an address and person of contact. Same thing goes for homeowners, the information is registered at the deeds of record office. This also helps you see how many employees, or how much money is invested in that entity. For example, if you wanted to find building contractors to do construction cleanup, you could get an idea of who is all running the establishment before even calling the receptionist. Another tactic is ordering you some yard signs and flyers to hire someone to distribute it to a specific location or upcoming event. What this means is say there is an upcoming event and you are wanting to sell a product. Someone passing out that information dressed accordingly can be hired to spread the word. An opportunity of mentioning is so you could call an employment agency or place the job on an employment database to provide the description for the job and pay. When you get a call for the job, setup an interview either phone, or video so you can see if this person would be a good fit for the job. The flipside to this is if you were to use a temp agency this is already completed. Again, another business opportunity that requires services for customers like you. Once you get someone out to the job of course they have to get paid accordingly. Which is essentially choosing payroll, cash, or commission. Commission tends to carry a less employee turnover financial loss, because you are giving them a percentage of what your getting. Taking your time starting out is the best approach in starting your own business with hiring anyone because you want to make sure your business is going in a steady direction. Which makes your business more successful in the long wrong because employees are consistently providing a service for you. Now if it were a product you were selling commission is safer to start with as well. Overall, when it comes to the hustle of expanding business income, paying employees goes a lot smoother with a payroll service.

Payroll to expanding

What are the benefits of setting up payroll? Payroll does a number of things, it helps relieve the process of paying your employee in cash for one. Also, who you hire, that receives payroll will show on credit report as their occupation. Even if you are a child the government states a child can work but cannot make up to a certain amount of money annually. Which is really good if your wanting to establish credit for your child before they turn of age. This in the long run is also helpful when leaving your business to your children. The business can build equity in it if you or the person in control of your assets can sell the business it could be a large payout. Or it could just continue to make profit. Your child can also be put on payroll and be an authorized user on the business credit card. This is what allows the child's credit score to be high by the time they turn 18. Of course, you would have to get approved for a business or personal credit card first, then put your child as an authorized user on that account. That way if your child wants to start a business in their name it will not be as hard since credit is already built up. Let's not forget the benefit of being able to go out and get a new car, apartment or house in their name because of perfect credit score. But always' keep a monitor of their credit report as well just in case someone tries to steal their identity.

On a side note, everyone needs good credit these days, unless you have a lot of money. The restriction to a child working is the specific job itself because, of safety laws and as long as the child does not make a over the amount of money a child is permitted to make. The IRS has a certain limit that a child cannot make over in a year. Use extreme caution in this part because you do not want to ruin your child's credit, so ensure you get a card you spend on one thing. For example, paying the electric bill, gas, rent, or lease whatever is something you cannot live without that is a small bill of course. That way you are paying back priority expenses you would have had to pay anyway. Instead of unnecessary spending that could lead in to a constant debt. Although, it's hard to escape debt, an account of spending in a excel sheet creates a transparency of conscious awareness. You become in control of making sure your business is making a profit and essentially reducing liabilities. Liabilities is anything that is can cause a risk to the business financial or debt obligation. When it comes to putting your child on small tasks or as you hire an employee, along with having worker's compensation insurance to cover your employees, if not through a temp agency, customers rely on a business having insurance and bonded for reassurance.

Getting your business insured and bonded is a brand itself. I tend to trust the branding of these names depending on the business of course. If you intend to provide services getting your business insured is almost as cheap as renters insurance. If the going rate is still under $50 dollars a month. This is not the same for selling online. Selling online typically does not require insurance or bonded unless of course it depends on what product your selling and if it meets FDA regulations. For instance, if you wanted to sell a beverage you were making in your house you may want to ensure you meet the guidelines for labeling and delivering nationwide. I remember a time I was doing a ride share, I picked a male in his mid-thirties up. He tells me about a friend of his that created a juice, had someone create a landing page specifically for the product to be purchased and was ordered abundantly. That he had made almost 100,000 that year. I'm not sure how true it is, but it does sound as if it could possibly happen. At bay, getting legal advice is necessary in this case to ensure no laws are being broken if you are ever unsure of what your selling. Labeling of the bottles and purchasing ingredients for inventory has become easier to manufacture and sell online. For example, if you wanted to start a lip gloss business, you can obtain the containers conduct labeling and shipping from home! Not to mention the instruction on how to make it is on the internet. Although it is simpler to sell certain products online, must of those products are much rather purchased in person. So always know how the customers goes about buying the product you are trying to sell. There's nothing worse then, watching inventory not sell.

Now that you have met the safety of protecting your business, finding the customers is the next step. Depending if you are meeting people face to face depends on the uniform or location of the business. There are many ways to run a business from anywhere actually. Even if you live in another country, as long as you are a us citizen you are able to register that business from another planet if you will. There are probably even virtual addresses that you can purchase, unbelievably.

I believe the hard part is having a in-state address for registering the business or essentially getting around that by seeing what exceptions are being made for outside us citizens seeking to register their business. Again, it may depend upon the state you choose to register. Registering the business simply is the professional thing to do. Especially, if you intend to do good business. Although there's nothing wrong with a business at home. You can grow a simple garden and say perhaps sell the products at a flea market. This is called Cottage food operations. If you know how to make jam or bake bread from scratch or other non-perishable foods or items, would fall under this examination. Check with your state's cottage food law. Most states have specifications on selling certain foods or products from the home due to certain zoning laws. Or if when selling vegetables overtime if you have the space to grow and protect your profits, getting a contract with a grocery store to supply vegetables is how farming essentially operates.

Economic shift in business

Over the years as business grows, a key thing to remember is hiring a manager to run the business so you can handle other important things like seeking new accounts. A manager takes on the responsibility of reporting the success of business to the owner. Or another fortunate alternative would be utilizing labor ready temp agencies for immediate employees. Especially, if you receive more contracts than you anticipate to a specified contract. That way you can accomplish the tasks quicker. So, essentially, employees are life lines to the business. Almost like branches of a tree. It permits the owner of the company to expand operations more smoothly.

Lets' say for example you have a business selling clothes. If the profits increase beyond the overhead costs of running the business, then you are making progress. Possibly, even relocating to other cities that have a higher demand. So, that you may affiliate yourself in to a brand competitor, expanding only creates a higher demand. If you have noticed when a product is released on the market. Once enough people have purchased the item off the shelves, the price reduces. My theory is that the business has made back their profit and are now thinking of a new product to market. Which is called a return on investment (ROI). This word is used allot when making deals, you always want to know what the return of putting your money into so something would profit you.

If you were to also travel to another country and you need someone to run the business, there are ways to top that hurdle acquiring a manager. Quite frankly, it has become more desirable to work remotely for most. With the help of tech savvy developers, you can pretty much log in to a specific security software system to keep an eye on business operations. Which is a great business invention that was patented and created by a developer, so that we can stay more connected to the business operation, from employees to manager to customers. Soon the only people that will be on the road will be delivery, ride sharing, and contractors on the road. Most healthcare agencies are even expanding their operations in the home to more disabled citizens who are limited to back and forth doctor visits and checkups. As a business owner, everyday note businesses continue to thrive and fail, cities become more congested, diseases tend to spread rapidly next thing you know prices go up. The notion of staying indoors seems safer as towns begin overcrowding, if you ask me. Next thing you know we're in a saturation of businesses seeking innovation to stay current and competitive is almost like a seis pool. But the key to running your business successfully is adapting and staying aware to change in the economy. Because if there is an epic event that may disrupt the business you always want to be one of the first to be prepared. For example, if you hear about a product that is trending, you may can acquire that item to selling from your online or local store.

Adapting to change allows the business to stand firm. Technology changes, customers age, and prices fluctuate, and new development changes the narrative. More people tend to spend more time on the phone then face to face conversation. Nothing wrong with that, it happens with the fascination of technology. However, this changes the game to creating targeted ads online depending on if you're selling a product or if you're selling a service in a local area. Reason being, a service is more effective with local advertising versus social media for instance. Local newspapers, and community boards and targeted customers should only get the buzz. If the business was expanding stores nationwide, then branding on social media would be a good benefit. You want more people to remember the name is the selling tactic of branding.

A simple Instagram page of what your business can be effective. Over time you will need to improve the quality of your services and it will take a lot of your time to grow the social media page. You should not have to worry too much about getting likes and shares because again it depends on if your selling online or selling a service. Now if you're selling a product then shares and likes and branding on social media is a good benefit. However, you still may want to have just a business page without revealing the owner. It just leaves out the questionable impression a customer may perceive. For instance, certain actions make customers not like your product just because they may not like you. It just rules out the possibility of any rumors.

Finally, the moment you been waiting for, the script. You must know and have your own script written down. The premise for this, is so you will be able to address callers concerns or needs for your service in order to save the customers time. There are ways to setup an IVR so that callers have to select certain prompts to get to you. Especially, if it's just you starting out answering the phone. There are a number of services that will provide an IVR system for your business phone with a personal professional greeting specific to what you want your callers to hear. So, when you do answer calls, or they leave a message you will have a better understanding of what the customer called to inquiry about. Another reason to have a script is what if someone wants to know about the costs or your mission anything. You want to be ready is what the script does. Don't get me wrong soon you will not need a script it will be programmed.

Business checklist

In a nutshell, once you design the business name and logo using word or paying for a freelancer to design it, you must register the name selected on the state website that you want to do business in. In either your name, Doing Business As or LLC.

(Cost of registering the business name + cost of (DBA) fee, and to run it in a local paper is inexpensive and it depends on the state. An ad in the local paper is required to announce the Fictitious name for a DBA. An LLC is simply just registering the LLC and placing your Articles along with your LLC.

1. Get a business number or 800 number online.
2. Apply for an EIN number on the IRS website.
3. Make sure you get a business tax license after you get your EIN at the county tax office in the area you want to do business.

(Which can also both be done simultaneously online with a credit card after registering the business. If you are a veteran or depending on tax credit in some states, you could qualify for an exempt. Which means you could go from county to county and essentially expand if your waived the county tax.)

4. Apply to have your business verified on the internet in Google creates trust on all platforms.
5. Create your mission of who you are and list your services in the website.
6. Setup LinkedIn page/ or a business social media account (not personal).

7. Setup your email account and insert logo in signature box.
8. Purchase same day standard business cards.

(*This can also be purchased online after selecting the theme of the business card. You want to keep the card simple and not include your name, because when customers call their more than likely will either speak to you or a virtual receptionist.*)

9. Setup a business bank account.
10. Get a name badge made as an account rep or sales rep and a couple of T-shirts or Polo shirts for your business.

(*When you need to hire, setup a payroll system through a small business so that employees can be paid by the day or by the week. This is not something you have to rush and do per say.*)

11. Last but not the least, once the website is verified (5 days), start posting ads online, creating, and passing out flyers to get the word out to the customers that are going to need your business. (If you decide to go with pamphlets it's no harm done, just know that the purpose is to leave them as a take home for reading material). When you get a call to go out on a job bring a form with you to take notes so that you are aware of the specifics of what a customer needs before providing an estimate of the cost of services.

(*Unless your selling products online you do not need to register the business nor as an LLC nor purchase a badge and shirt.*)

A strong marketing ad although may seem like a challenge, running local ads, flyers, yard signs will get any business up and running. The fastest way to get customers is to post ads and build awareness so people can remember your business name. Leaving yard signs and posting flyers is a sure way of getting customers to take advantage of a sale or offering. It is hard to imagine someone passing out flyers just to talk about their business. It could create a bad image for the business if too many people throw it away. If it's just you and your providing a service, its best to wear your company shirt and a badge so customers learn to adapt to the name and not you as an individual. As the business grows you may need an accountant to ensure the business keeps record of all expenses for taxes.

What you need to know about marketing on social media? Depending on your search results and what you typically follow determines the specific ads for you. What this means, is that every ad that you see whether commercial or online, is specifically targeted to your demographic content. Companies are knowing and building more efficient software to target the leads of the customers habit. Reason for this, is so businesses legally find customers specifically for their service or product. Let's be honest how else does something only you are searching for appears in many of the ads you see. So essentially, knowing what content you are designed to see gives you more control over the things you are interested in.

When it comes to the anxiety of marketing ads to a specific demographic, there are ways to get around the dreadful rejection. When it came time for me to start my business. I knew I had the knowledge of how to get started. Of course, depending on how much money you have to spend on getting started will depend on the alternate ways of avoiding rejection. What many owners of a business may do, is hire a business manager or someone to handle or run the business. They way to go about this is arranging a salary ideal to the specific business description. For instance, if I just needed to hire someone to call and make appointments, for a simple 5 hours a day the calls you have will be the required commission you can set to pay. If an assistant makes 20 to 30 calls a day, provided they have the leads and contacts, only 10 of the leads would turn a profit for you. The next step would just be to advertise for a sales representative to meet with the client or customer, that is if it's a service. In some cases, even if it's a service there's still a product being sold.

Commission to break even

So, how do you go about finding a sales representative? Well, just like observing the trend, just look at an example of a job position ad. Depending on your community, you can even leave flyers in certain organizations or locations for people seeking to make extra money on the side. What this does is builds an employee base. Again, using an example is always the best way to get started. Unlike big corporations that partner with an ad agency to continue making ads for the company. Which works best for a company that may continuously sell a variety of products. So far, this is only as a business gets bigger, unless you have another way to arrange a partnership with an ad agency at the startup of the business. Since business involves the exchange of goods or services, arranging a partnership or payment schedule for a person or another company to assist in profits. Is very popular.

Hiring a sales representative can be moderately simple depending on the business, if you will. Especially, if the hours of business may vary. Most sales representatives get paid by commission. Depending on what you base that sales commission on is what that person receives for landing the sale. A 1099, a check or direct deposit can pay the sales representative at the convenience of the person desire way to get paid. And if you get paid on the job that means at a consistent weekly schedule you are in business. Payroll services is what handles the process for you. You just deposit the amount in the bank and the payroll service process the transaction to get paid on a specific date. At the end of the year you can print off your annual sheet to file your taxes or hire a tax preparer. Of course, this is a business expense the more employees you hire, the more business, the more profit. This can be an amazing way to relieve your responsibilities and just monitor their performance. It really just takes the discipline of being consistent. And if you look at it, it's identical to working a regular job. Even when you don't feel like going you go with the paralyzed thought to simply get it over with. Keep in mind that when hiring employees there is always a chance of an injury or incident so workers comp most likely would be required to protect your asset.

Now you may question your success in business. With the thought of do I actually need employees. The answer is, it depends. For instance, if you were to open a commercial cleaning business as a sole proprietor or LLC, you may get a call for a larger contract cleaning. In which could not be possibly sought by one person. So, you may have to be in the position to hire people. Now say you want to execute other contracts while you have one contract already being conducted. This would be the time to either hire a person to do a walkthrough of the cleaning or you can do it after the cleaners have left for the day/night.

The question is not whether you want employees it's whether you want to expand. Cause if you think about it visually in pretense. If you were to receive an assignment that could possibly take a week to resolve (hypothetically speaking if you were to have a cleaning business), in-between that time you can accomplish new assignments.

Objective summary

The hardest part of running a business is the three C's. Commitment, consistency, and care. Applying all three of these characteristics as a business owner, you will develop a learned behavior of the three C's. Especially, when your faced with personal or health problems, your business is basically your life. Now you can see why many positions become available for the participation of running a business. Which is initially executing the mission of a business. Just think about it, how many times do you call a customer care representative and the first greeting is the business mission along with thanking you for calling. Don't get me wrong if you were to call a receptionist or secretary, which is essentially the same job, you will get an option to select a specific department. Let me remind you, this too is an IVR system set up for each phone. The exact same thing an entrepreneur or small business owner can succeed.

As long as you keep in mind anyone can register their business as long as you meet the requisite to do such. Primarily it is obtaining the legal right to do business. After this task, it's pretty much getting the county license to do business, which can have exemption (waiver) for certain individuals. There are some business services, or contractors that may not need a visual or delightful website. For example, a post commercial cleanup business. Contractors and home owners to referrals are simply looking for a good clean. So, having an exquisite website may not be so impressive to customers. However, nowadays with the internet, you can simply create a drop shipping business within a day.

Allow me to share with you my experience with that. I once watched a video about opening an online store. Next thing you know, an ad appears, simply stating that you can buy or auction other drop shipping websites. The research in me had to do my Sherlock Holmes and seek out the truth in this hypocrisy. Turns out there is a website that actually allows website owners to auction or sell their drop shipping store. Completely in shock, I began seeking for transparency in the success of purchasing a drop shipping business. If you were to search for these keywords of purchasing drop shipping websites, you should be able to see the same opportunity. Establishing more traffic and perhaps a little editing to touch up newer items is the minimum needed to jump right in. As I mentioned before, marketing ads on social media for about 5 bucks a day can create traffic and create leads as well. Try picturing in your mind, a customer sees an ad talking about an exciting offer, while their spending time scrolling on social media. What happens is that person then clicks on that ad. Which then sends you to a landing page. A landing page is essentially another URL, redirecting you to a call to action. A call to action is simply probing the person to leave specific inquiry, request, or data in order for the person to receive the information they are seeking. It can be as simple as a form or another website to a blog or store. The purpose of putting a landing page is so that if someone click on a link and it goes to another website. Unless there is exclusive content, that person can perhaps back out of the website. Thus, losing a potential client.

Online selling indeed is becoming a variable passive income. Even if you have no interest in what your selling there is always a specific customer base seeking those items. Not only that, you will have the liberty to develop multiple pages. Most of the time your theme will allow you to just add another page. The biggest revenue of making money online is utilizing Google Ad Sense. Ensuring that you setup an account, allows other ad placement for your website thus creating more revenue just in case the person that visits your page finds something else interesting. We'll say shopping for a sale another item. This term is used loosely as affiliate networking. Many websites and stores allow this option, thus creating an entire website of click bait.

Conclusion

In conclusion, there are essentially 11 steps to get your business started. Even if you were seeking to just get an investor to invest in your idea, marketing to investors would be the same tactic as seeking customers. Not all businesses that are offline may not require a certain insurance, so it's best to ensure you get the correct coverage for your business. Just as you would your house or apartment. Make certain that you practice your approach or your appearance that you want others to declare you as a business owner. Which only takes the confirmation that if anything was to happen you are covered no matter if it's just a simple refund or exchange. Even if you were to seek creating a channel, marketing your channel is the best way to ensure you reach the potential crowd that would be interested in watching your channel. Which can be done by setting the search words identical to a popular search already in progress. For instance, if you type in a search for a video, warrant that you place the keywords the same as it was typed. Granting you a position in the world of algorithm, which is the amount of times your keywords are searched. Always keep your website updated. Keep in touch with leads by creating a way to capture their email. If you need emails to start off without asking and revealing you are the owner, you can simply see your friends' email on social media at times.

At first it may seem like you are going to fail, just keep in mind even the best businesses experience slow money days. This is all the time you need to reflect on what ways you can remain competitive. As you learned in school, watching what others are doing is a great way to get better at your craft.

Recap:

Always be accountable of tax laws, so that you can keep account of what income brackets get taxed the most, what the tax rate is you would have to pay, how you can pay it and why if any would you face any tax problems.

Service agreements or contract templates can also be found on the internet for free depending on where you look or pay a freelancer experienced in that category to simply put one together.

There are fill in the blank software for creating service agreements that allow you to insert the name and date accordingly so you can keep a standard service agreement. Another way depending on the business you are wanting to start, a paralegal can assist if you're not on a tight budget or the internet may have a free template to use to ensure you have a professional agreement, or contract ready to give to customers or clients.

Call local newspapers for ad pricing to get to the community or area your seeking to find customers in to weigh out your options on the costs and which newspaper is the best.

Keep track of business expenses as to how much money you spend on advertising getting supplies, software and anything that requires the business to successfully run for tax preparation.

It may help to get large envelopes or some sort of file sorter, so you can just stuff everything from that month (receipts, invoices, statements, etc.) or client information in that specific envelope.

Keep in mind once you register your business, there are people that will solicit their services to assist your business in getting started up, or they will scam you if you do not know the following steps to become a legitimate business in which this book details.

All results may vary because the number one reason businesses fail is lack of customers and commitment.